P9-DTQ-831

DRINKING GAMES

photography by William Lingwood

DRINKING GAMES

TERRY BURROWS

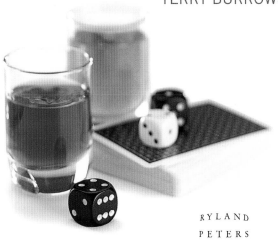

RYLAND
PETERS
& SMALL

LONDON NEW YORK

Senior Designer Paul Tilby
Editor Rachel Lawrence
Production Simon Walsh
Art Director Anne-Marie Bulat
Publishing Director Alison Starling

Stylist Liz Belton
Indexer Hilary Bird

First published in the USA in 2006
by Ryland Peters & Small, Inc.
519 Broadway, 5th Floor
New York NY 10012
www.rylandpeters.com

10 9 8 7 6 5 4 3 2

Text, design, and photographs
© Ryland Peters & Small 2006

ISBN-10: 1 84597 278 3
ISBN-13: 978 1 84597 278 3

Library of Congress Cataloging-in-
Publication Data

Burrows, Terry.
  Drinking games / Terry Burrows ; pho-
tography by William Lingwood.
      p. cm.
  Includes index.
  ISBN-13: 978-1-84597-278-3
  ISBN-10: 1-84597-278-3
  1. Drinking games. I. Lingwood,
William. II. Title.
  GV1202.D74.B87 2006
  793.2--dc22

2006012382

Printed and bound in China

contents

let the games begin

Throughout history, alcohol has fuelled a vast array of varied functions. It's been used in worship, and widely appreciated for its medicinal and antiseptic properties. But its most vital role has surely been in enhancing the enjoyment and quality of our lives—whether as relaxant, social lubricant, or simply as a purveyor of pharmacological delight.

We can reasonably guess that the (presumably) accidental discovery of the merits of drinking fermented malt or grapes would have been followed not long after by a conga line around the field. However, it was not until the time of the Ancient Romans that we have the first recorded proof of the existence of drinking games. These were not sophisticated. One of the most popular was based around the rapid consumption of cups of wine, the number dictated by the throw of a die, often—according to accounts from the period—followed by induced vomiting, thus enabling consumption of yet more alcohol.

Of course, we live in altogether more enlightened times and now know that the key to enjoying alcohol is moderation. The games selected here are guaranteed to enhance any liquid social gathering, some of them require a degree of manual dexterity and some are actually quite urbane parlor games—and others are, frankly, idiotic! That said, alcohol is, of course, one of life's great levelers, and the smartest guy in the room will suddenly look the biggest fool when screaming out: "Two frogs, eight legs, four eyes, in a pond, Splash! Splash!" after three or four beers.

So, fill your glasses and prepare for action.

Cheers!

WORDS

initial thoughts

PLAYERS: as many as possible

One player makes up a question to which everyone else must give a two-word answer. The tough part is that the answer must begin with the initials of their own name. Players are allowed a maximum of five seconds to respond. If they fail to answer, or give a poor or incorrect response, they must pay a drinking forfeit. That player then becomes the question master for the next round. Here is an example with four players:

Question master:	*"Name a type of food"*
Frank Price:	*"Fried potatoes"*
Bill Carson:	*"Boiled carrots"*
Francis Seaton:	*"Fresh seaweed"*
Frank Price:	*"Fish pâté"*
Bill Carson:	*"Bread and cheese"*

word association

PLAYERS: **as many as possible**

The contestants sit around a table. One player is nominated the judge, and says the first word that comes into his or her head.

Moving clockwise around the circle, the next player has to respond with a word that is in some way linked to the first word. Play continues in the same manner. Any player failing to give an immediate or appropriate response must pay a drinking forfeit; play then moves to the next player in the circle. At any point, the judge may ask a player to justify his or her link to the previous word—if the judge rejects the explanation, the player must pay the forfeit. Here is an example of some associations:

Judge:	*"Tea"*
Player one:	*"Coffee"*
Player two:	*"Brazil"*
Player three:	*"Jungle"*
Player four:	*"Monkey"*
Player five:	*"Tree"*

keep it clean

PLAYERS: any number

This cunning tongue-twister is possibly not one to be played with prospective in-laws or your local minister within earshot.

Players sit in a circle. The first player shouts out *"Fuzzy Duck."*

The next person clockwise in the circle can respond either by saying (i) *"Fuzzy Duck"* or (ii) *"Does he?"* If it is (i), play continues clockwise, with the next player given the same options; if it is (ii), play continues counter-clockwise, with the next player given the option of shouting *"Ducky Fuzz"* or *"Does he?"* If it is the latter, play changes direction again.

It may sound simple, but as the game speeds up things can quickly get out of hand. Any player speaking out of turn or giving the wrong response pays a drinking forfeit.

To summarize: When play is moving clockwise it's *"Fuzzy Duck"* or *"Does he?"* When play is moving counter-clockwise it's *"Ducky Fuzz"* or *"Does he?"*

banished letters

The aim of the game is to answer questions without using a specified letter of the alphabet.

The MC first decides which letter is to be banned. He or she then sets a question to each of the players in turn. Their answers must not contain the forbidden letter anywhere in the word, or repeat a previous answer. The first player whose answer uses that letter—or who fails to give a correct answer—pays a drinking forfeit. That player then becomes MC for the next round of the game. Here is an example:

MC:	*"The forbidden letter is S. Name a US state."*
Player one:	*"New York"*
Player two:	*"California"*
Player three:	*"Montana"*
Player four:	*"Texas"*

Player four pays a drinking forfeit and becomes MC for the next round.

14 WORDS

famous names

PLAYERS: as many as possible, sitting around a table

DRINKS: each player should have the same amount (since this game requires continuous consumption, it's best played with beer rather than wine or—heaven forbid!—spirits)

Player one nominates a subject that describes a specific group of famous people. For example: "Country singers" or "American rock groups."

The next player clockwise must take a sip of drink—however small—before responding with an appropriate example. Play continues in this way around the circle.

However, while a player is drinking and thinking the other players may also shout out appropriate examples. These may then not be used in the game, thus forcing the player to continue drinking while trying to come up with something original.

tell the truth

PLAYERS: **any number**

DRINKS: **before you start, agree a unit of measurement to be used as a forfeit—a shot glass of beer, for example**

Player one begins by making a declaration about a deed which they have NEVER done. This might be something like: *"I have never been to Paris"* or *"I have never eaten sushi."* Or perhaps something more risqué.

Any player who HAS done this deed must pay a single drinking forfeit.

Any player denying they have done the deed, but who is known by another player to have done it, must pay two forfeits.

Any player who claims to have done the deed, but who is not believed by everyone else, pays the severest penalty of all—four forfeits.

Be VERY careful who you choose as your fellow players!

rhyme or reason

The first player says any word that comes into his or her head. The next person clockwise in the circle must then either come up with a word that RHYMES with the previous word, or one that DESCRIBES what it does.

For example, if player one says *"Cat"*, player two might offer *"Bat"* or *"Purr"* as a response. Anyone failing to come up with an adequate word must take a drink and then start the game afresh with a new word.

To make things more challenging, you can impose a time limit of five·seconds on coming up with an answer.

if I had a …

PLAYERS: as many as possible, sitting in a circle

This may be the simplest drinking game ever, and yet after a few drinks it can be surprisingly difficult.

Players gather in a circle. One person begins by saying "If I had a …" and then adds a random word of his or her own choosing. The game then moves around the circle, players adding one word at a time with the aim of creating a free-flowing sentence. Any player who hesitates, can't think of a word, or says something that makes no grammatical sense pays a drinking forfeit. Here is an example:

Player one:	*"If I had a fish …"*
Player two:	*"… I'd …"*
Player three:	*" … wear …"*
Player four:	*" … it …"*
Player five:	*" … on …"*
Player one:	*" … my …"*
Player two:	*" … head …"*

froggy splash

PLAYERS: **the more the better, sitting in a circle**

One person begins by saying the following phrase:
"One frog, four legs, two eyes, in a pond, SPLASH!"

Player two responds with:
"Two frogs, eight legs, four eyes, in a pond, SPLASH! SPLASH!"

Player three then says:
"Three frogs, twelve legs, six eyes, in a pond, SPLASH! SPLASH! SPLASH!"

Player four responds with:
"Four frogs, sixteen legs, eight eyes, SPLASH! SPLASH! SPLASH! SPLASH!"

The game continues in this manner, with the number of frogs, legs, eyes, and splashes correctly adjusted each time. Any player making a mistake pays a drinking forfeit, and play passes to the next player in the circle.

ACTIONS

fish face

This is a simple word game that inevitably ends up with uncontrollable laughter—even if everyone is sober.

Players sit in a circle and each selects the name of a type of fish. No two players may have the same fish.

The first player says: *"I'm a ... (his or her fish name); you're a ... (someone else's fish name.)"* That player must repeat the phrase, inserting his own name and that of another player. Play continues in this way.

However, to make things more interesting, contestants have to talk without showing their teeth! Anyone giving even the briefest glimpse of tooth has to pay a drinking forfeit.

slappers

PLAYERS: **any number, sitting around a table**

Players sit in a circle with their hands flat on the table top. An MC is nominated (he or she doesn't take part in the round.)

The game begins when the person clockwise from the MC slaps their left hand and then their right hand down on the table. Play continues to proceed clockwise, the next player slapping his or her hands on the table in the same manner. However, at any time during the game, the MC may choose to give signals altering the course of play:

• A clap from the MC means that play changes direction.

• Two claps means that the order in which the hands are slapped must be reversed.

• Three claps means that players must also shout out the opposite hand to the one they are slapping down.

• Four claps mean that play stops while all players take a swig.

Whenever a player makes a mistake, a forfeit of a single swig of drink must be paid. Each time play stops in this way, a new MC takes over—this should be the next person sitting clockwise.

riotous relay

PLAYERS: two teams of equal numbers

DRINKS: each player must have a full glass of his or her chosen beverage

Players on each team stand in a line. Everyone shouts out the countdown—***"Three, two, one, GO!"***—upon which the first player in each team proceeds to down their drink as quickly as possible, placing the empty glass on his or her head. This is the cue for the second player in the team to begin drinking.

The winning team is the one that finishes its drinks the quickest.

spray time

PLAYERS: **the more the better**

DRINKS: **one can of beer is needed per player;
the cans should all be identical**

Place all of the cans of beer in a bag. One can is then pulled out at random, given a vigorous shaking, and then placed back in the bag. Make sure you mix the cans around in the bag so that the shaken one is "lost" among the others.

Each player then closes his or her eyes and pulls out a drink from the bag. With the opening pointing toward their faces, on a count of three everyone opens their can.

One unlucky player will be covered in an explosion of frothing beer.

If there is a large number of players, the cans can be placed on a table instead of in a bag.

Younger players can also enjoy this game using cans of fizzy soft drink.

matchbox mayhem

PLAYERS: **two players**

REQUIREMENTS: **two empty matchboxes, two glasses of beer; before you start, agree a unit of measurement to be used as a forfeit**

Players sit facing each other, both with a beer glass resting between their thighs. The object of the game is for each player, in turn, to try to flick their matchbox into their opponent's glass. Whenever one succeeds, their opponent must pay a drinking forfeit.

However, if the opponent responds successfully, then the drinking forfeit is doubled and passed back to the other player. This cumulative forfeit may continue until one player misses. Here is an example:

Player one:	scores
Player two:	scores (and so doesn't have to pay single forfeit)
Player one:	scores (and so doesn't have to pay double forfeit)
Player two:	scores (and so doesn't have to pay triple forfeit)
Player one:	misses (must pay triple forfeit)

tune time

A nominated player comes up with a single-word subject for the game. Each player must take it in turn to sing an extract from a song that includes the chosen word. Any player failing to come up with a song, or who sings something which has already been selected (or just sings especially badly), must pay a drinking forfeit. Here is an example to get you started:

Subject:	**Rock**
Player one:	*"We're gonna rock around the clock tonight ..."*
Player two:	*"I love rock 'n' roll ..."*
Player three:	*"Rock of ages ..."*

drinking with the simpsons

PLAYERS: two or more

This game is played while watching an episode of "The Simpsons."

Variations on this game exist (or can be created) for almost any cult movie or TV show. The rules are simple: you take a drink EVERY TIME any of the following happens:

- Homer says "D'oh!"
- Homer says "Mmmmm… " (take two drinks if it's over a non-edible object)
- Homer eats a donut
- Homer is seriously injured
- Bart says "Aye Caramba!"
- Marge groans
- Maggie sucks on her pacifier
- Mr. Burns says "Excellent!"
- Principal Skinner makes a 'Nam reference
- Comic Book Guy makes a sarcastic remark

CARDS

the fourth jack

PLAYERS: **three or more**
REQUIREMENTS: **a deck of playing cards**

This is a fine game for getting an evening started.

The cards are shuffled and placed face down on the table. Players take it in turn to draw the top card from the pack and show it to the group. The first player to draw a jack is asked to nominate a type of beer. The second player to draw a jack names a type of spirit. The player turning over the third jack then has to go to the bar and buy the two drinks. The player drawing the fourth jack has to drink them!

cards on heads

PLAYERS: **three or more**
REQUIREMENTS: **a deck of playing cards**

This is a variation on the famous "names on heads" party game.

The cards are shuffled and one is dealt, face down, to each player. That card must then be swiftly held against the player's forehead so that he or she does not know what it is, but everyone else in the group does.

The object of the game is for each player to bet on whether they think their card is the highest one. Bets are made in units of drink, up to a maximum of five. When the cards are revealed, all of the losing players must drink whatever the winner bid, plus their own individual bets.

crossing the bridge

PLAYERS: **three or more**
REQUIREMENTS: **a deck of playing cards**

Deal out a line of five cards, face down—this is the "bridge."

Turn the first card. If it is a number, you are free to turn over the next card. If, however, a face card appears you must pay a drinking forfeit accordingly: the jack is one unit; queen is two; king is three, and ace is four. You must also add the same number of new cards face down to the end of the bridge. When you have reached the end of the bridge, the next player takes his or her turn. Here is an example:

Action:	Deal five cards, face down; turn card one
Card one:	Three of clubs
Action:	Turn card two
Card two:	Seven of diamonds
Action:	Turn card three
Card three:	Queen of spades
Action:	Take two units of drink; add two cards to the end of the bridge; turn card four …

feeling left out

PLAYERS: **any number**
REQUIREMENTS: **a deck of playing cards, some small objects**

Select four cards of a kind for each player from the deck. In the middle of the table there should be a number of small objects, such as coins, pens, matches, lighters, etc. There should be ONE LESS object than the number of players.

Deal the pack so that each player has four cards. The object of the game is to collect four cards of a kind. Each player then studies their cards and tries to pass on one unwanted card to the player on their left. Each player looks at their new card and decides whether to pass it on or exchange it for one of their own cards.

The game continues in this way until one player has four of a kind. He or she then grabs one of the objects from the table. This is the signal for everyone else to follow suit. The player left empty-handed has to pay a drinking forfeit before re-joining the game.

40 CARDS

cops and robbers

PLAYERS: **four or more, sitting around a large table**
REQUIREMENTS: **a deck of playing cards**

The number of cards required is the same as the number of people playing. Take one ace and one king and make the remainder up from cards with a value of two, three, four, and five. Shuffle the cards and deal one, face down, to each player.

Whoever receives the king is the cop; the ace is the robber. Their identities remain hidden. The robber must make a deal with one of the players by giving them a wink. That player then says: ***"The deal has been made."*** (Previously, everyone will have been looking around the table for the wink, and the cop is on alert to try to catch the robber in the act.)

Once "the deal has been made," the cop makes him- or herself known, and tries to guess who the robber is. If the cop guesses wrong, he or she has to drink the same number of drinks as the value of the accused's card. This continues until the cop identifies the robber. If the robber happens to wink at the cop, he or she is automatically busted and has to drink a number of drinks.

suits you

PLAYERS: **any number**

REQUIREMENTS: **a deck of playing cards and four large glasses, two containing an alcoholic drink, two containing a soft drink; there should be enough of each drink to refill glasses as they become empty**

Remove the four kings and place one alongside each of the full glasses—this designates the suit for each glass. Shuffle the pack and place it on the table, face down.

The first player draws a card from the the top of the deck. He or she must then drink from the glass designated by the suit, for the number of seconds indicated by the card. Jacks count as eleven seconds; queens as twelve seconds. An ace means that everyone else must drink from the designated glass for five seconds.

For example if spades are designated as beer; clubs, gin and tonic; hearts, orange juice; and diamonds, water, a player who draws the six of clubs must drink from the gin and tonic glass for six seconds.

circle of chance

PLAYERS: as many as possible, sitting in a circle
REQUIREMENTS: two decks of playing cards

Take the two decks of cards and shuffle them together into a single pile. Competitors gather in a circle. The first person draws a card from the top of the pile. Moving clockwise, the second player draws the next card from the pile. If the two cards are the same suit, both players must pay a single drinking forfeit; if the cards are of the same numerical value, both players must drink that amount. If the cards are not matching, the game moves on to player three, who draws a card which is matched against that of player two.

waste the ace

PLAYERS: **any number, sitting around a table**
REQUIREMENTS: **a deck of playing cards**

This game requires the same number of cards as there are players.
If there are fewer than 13, take out a single suit and select them
numerically from ace upwards.

Players gather in a circle. Each one is dealt a playing card face
down on the table in front of them. One at a time, each player
looks at his or her card and decides whether to keep it or swap
it with the player on the left. The loser, who must pay a drinking
forfeit, is the one with the lowest card (the ace) at the end of the
round. If you choose to swap, then you MUST keep the card
which is passed to you—the only way to get rid of it is if the
player on your right asks to swap with you.

the evil glass

PLAYERS: **three to eight, sitting in a circle; ideally, everybody should have a different drink—the more variety the better**

REQUIREMENTS: **a deck of playing cards, an empty glass, a thimble (or very small glass)**

The group sits in a circle with the deck of cards shuffled and placed face down and the empty pint glass ("the evil glass") in the middle.

The first player turns over a card. Remember the numerical value of this card (face cards count as ten)—it is the "magic number." That player then pours a thimble full of his or her own drink into the "evil glass."

The next person turns over a card and then pours some of their drink into the glass. Play continues around the circle in this way until someone turns over a card of the same numerical value as the magic number. That person must then drink the contents of the evil glass.

DICE & COINS

one in six

PLAYERS: **three or more**
REQUIREMENTS: **one die, five shot glasses filled with drinks**

Line up the shot glasses and number them from one to five.

All players roll the die—the highest score starts the game.

The rules are simple. In turn, players roll the die. If they throw between one and five, they drink the corresponding shot. If it is empty, they fill the shot glass with the drink of their choice. If someone throws a six, the next player clockwise in the circle must drink all of the remaining shots.

the clock game

PLAYERS: **any number**
REQUIREMENTS: **two dice**

The object of the game is for players to throw scores from 1 up to 12 in ascending numerical order. Scores can be achieved either from a single die or by totalling both dice.

Player one shakes the dice looking for a score of 1. If either die has a value of 1, then he or she rolls the dice again, this time hoping to see a 2. (If a double 1 is thrown at this point, then the spots on the two dice can be added together to give a score of 2.) The round ends when the player fails to score any more points— play then passes to the next player in line.

Every time one player achieves the next number in their sequence, all of the other players must take the same number of sips of their drink.

drop dead

PLAYERS: three or more
REQUIREMENTS: five dice

The first player rolls all five dice. If the dice do NOT show a 2 or a 5, the value of the spots is totalled and written on the scorecard. The first player takes a drink and then throws again with all five dice. If, however, any of the dice show a 2 or a 5, then the player scores 0, and those dice showing 2 or 5 are lost. This time ALL players must take a drink. Play continues with the remaining dice. The turn continues until the final die shows a 2 or a 5, at which point the score from each round is added, and play moves to the next player. The winner of the game is the one scoring the most points. Here is an example of play:

Throw 1:	2, 3, 6, 5, 4	(0 points, lose two dice)	
Throw 2:	6, 6, 6	(18 points)	
Throw 3:	2, 1, 4	(0 points, lose one die)	
Throw 4:	6, 4	(10 points)	
Throw 5:	2, 1	(0 points, lose one die)	
Throw 6:	2	(0 points, lose final die)	Total score: 28 points

the tower

PLAYERS: **three or more**
REQUIREMENTS: **one die, drinks suggested below, coasters**

This game requires a "tower" of drinks to be constructed. This is done by resting a coaster on the top of a glass, and balancing the next drink on that coaster. Suggested drinks are as follows, from top to bottom: shot of tequila, double vodka, gin and tonic, glass of red wine, beer.

Players sit in a circle and roll the die in turn. The first player to throw a six must drink the tequila. The second player rolling a six removes the coaster underneath. The third six drinks the vodka. The game continues until play reaches the beer.

An additional rule could be that while the beer is being drunk, the other players frantically take turns to throw a six—if they succeed, the player drinking the beer must pay for the next round of the game to be set up.

catch the pig

PLAYERS: **eight or more, sitting around a table**
REQUIREMENTS: **two dice**

All players sit around a table. One die is given to one player, the other to the player sitting directly opposite.

The game starts with everyone shouting *"Catch the Pig."* Players must then throw their dice. When a player throws a one, the die is passed to the next player on his or her left. Players take as many throws as are needed to score one—and as quickly as possible.

The object of the game is to catch up with the other player. When this happens, the game stops, and the person "caught" has to finish their drink.

counting coins

PLAYERS: **any number, sitting around a table**
REQUIREMENTS: **each player needs three coins**

Players hide their hands under the table and place either three, two, one, or no coins in one of their hands. This hand is then held closed above the table.

The object of the game is for each player to guess the total number of coins being held. When everyone has made a guess, all the players open their hands, and the coins are counted. Any player who guesses correctly is allowed to retire from the game; everyone else pays a drinking forfeit and plays another round. The game continues until only one person remains; that player must then buy the drinks for the next game.

coin soccer

PLAYERS: **two players (or two teams of equal numbers)**
REQUIREMENTS: **each player (or team) requires a "flicking" coin; a smaller coin for the "ball", two bottles for "goals"**

The two bottles (the "goals") are placed at either end of the area defined as the playing field. The "flicking" coins are placed alongside each bottle. The "ball" is placed in the middle of the field.

Players take it in turns to flick their own coins so that they hit the ball and gradually move it toward their opponent's goal. A goal is scored each time the ball strikes an opponent's bottle. When this happens, the player (or the entire team) conceding the goal must take a drink. If a flicking coin strikes the other player's coin before (or instead of) the ball, it is a foul. That player (not the team) is penalized with a drinking fine. Two free flicks are also given to the fouled player.

The game can be played for a set time or until an agreed number of goals have been scored. The losing team must then buy the drinks for the next game.

anchorman

PLAYERS: **two teams of equal numbers**
REQUIREMENTS: **a full pitcher of beer; each player requires a small coin**

The teams sit in a line on opposite sides of a table. The pitcher of beer stands in between. One player on each team is designated as the "anchorman."

One at a time, players from the first team attempt to flick their coins into the pitcher. They are only allowed one attempt per round. The second team then attempts to flick their coins into the pitcher. Play then returns to the first team. This time, however, only those who failed in the previous round play. The game continues in this manner until all of the players in one team have successfully shot their coins into the pitcher.

The losing team must drink the entire contents of the pitcher. Players may decide how much or little they drink; however, the "anchorman" always drinks last, and must finish off the pitcher.